budgetbooks

ACOUSTIC HITS

Exclusive Distributors:
Music Sales Limited
8/9 Frith Street, London W1D 3JB, UK.

Order No. HLE90002792
ISBN 1-84609-364-3
This book © Copyright 2005 by Hal Leonard Europe

Printed in the USA

Your Guarantee of Quality
As publishers, we strive to produce every book to the highest commercial standards.
The book has been carefully designed to minimise awkward page turns and to make playing from it a real pleasure.
Throughout, the printing and binding have been planned to ensure a sturdy, attractive publication which should give years of enjoyment.
If your copy fails to meet our high standards, please inform us and we will gladly replace it.

www.musicsales.com

This publication is not authorised for sale in the
United States of America and/or Canada

Hal Leonard Europe
Distributed by Music Sales

CONTENTS

4   Adia
Sarah McLachlan

16   Amanda
Boston

24   American Pie
Don McLean

34   And I Love Her
The Beatles

38   Annie's Song
John Denver

11   Baby, I Love Your Way
Peter Frampton

42   Barely Breathing
Duncan Sheik

48   Best Of My Love
The Eagles

60   Blackbird
The Beatles

53   Blaze Of Glory
Jon Bon Jovi

64   Blowin' In The Wind
Peter, Paul & Mary; Bob Dylan

68   Bus Stop
The Hollies

72   Can't Buy Me Love
The Beatles

76   Change The World
Eric Clapton

82   Come Monday
Jimmy Buffet

85   Crazy On You
Heart

94   Dear Prudence
The Beatles

99   Free Bird
Lynyrd Skynyrd

102   Girl
The Beatles

105   Have You Ever Really Loved A Woman?
Bryan Adams

110   Helplessly Hoping
Crosby, Stills & Nash

114   Her Town Too
James Taylor and J.D. Souther

122   Here Comes The Sun
The Beatles

127   Homeward Bound
Simon & Garfunkel

130   I Will
The Beatles

133   I'll Have To Say I Love You In A Song
Jim Croce

136   I'm Looking Through You
The Beatles

146   I've Just Seen A Face
The Beatles

141   If You Leave Me Now
Chicago

150   Julia
The Beatles

156   Just A Song Before I Go
Crosby, Stills & Nash

159   Leaving On A Jet Plane
Peter, Paul & Mary

162   Long Long Time
Linda Ronstadt

166   Lost In Love
Air Supply

170   Lovely Rita
The Beatles

184	Maggie May *Rod Stewart*		273	Small Town *John Mellencamp*
188	Me And Bobby McGee *Janis Joplin*		278	Southern Cross *Crosby, Stills & Nash*
200	Michelle *The Beatles*		286	Stay The Night *Chicago*
204	More Than Words *Extreme*		292	Summer Breeze *Seals & Crofts*
210	My Sweet Lord *George Harrison*		298	Sweet Talkin' Woman *Electric Light Orchestra*
175	Night Moves *Bob Seger & The Silver Bullet Band*		302	Take Me Home, Country Roads *John Denver*
218	Norwegian Wood (This Bird Has Flown) *The Beatles*		307	Tears In Heaven *Eric Clapton*
220	Nowhere Man *The Beatles*		312	Thing Called Love (Are You Ready For This Thing Called Love) *Bonnie Raitt*
224	Our House *Crosby, Stills, Nash & Young*		318	This Land Is Your Land *Woody & Arlo Guthrie*
232	Pink Houses *John Mellencamp*		320	Time In A Bottle *Jim Croce*
236	Poetry Man *Phoebe Snow*		324	Travelin' Man *Ricky Nelson*
248	Poor Little Fool *Ricky Nelson*		332	Until It's Time For You To Go *Elvis Presley*
241	Rocky Mountain High *John Denver*		327	Vincent (Starry Starry Night) *Don McLean*
250	Rocky Raccoon *The Beatles*		338	Wake Up Little Susie *The Everly Brothers*
264	Running On Faith *Eric Clapton*		342	Where Have All The Flowers Gone? *The Kingston Trio*
257	Show Me The Way *Peter Frampton*		345	Wonderwall *Oasis*
270	(Sittin' On) The Dock Of The Bay *Otis Redding*		350	Yesterday *The Beatles*

ADIA

Words and Music by SARAH McLACHLAN
and PIERRE MARCHAND

BABY, I LOVE YOUR WAY

Words and Music by
PETER FRAMPTON

AMANDA

Words and Music by
TOM SCHOLZ

AMERICAN PIE

Words and Music by
DON McLEAN

Man, I dig those rhy-thm and blues. _____ I was a lone-ly teen-age ___ bronc-in' buck __ with a pink car-na - tion and a pick-up truck. __ But I knew I ___ was out _____ of luck __ the day _ the mu - sic died. ___

day the mu - sic died. And they were sing - in'

this - 'll be the day ___ that I ___ die. ___

Additional Lyrics

2. Now for ten years we've been on our own,
   And moss grows fat on a rollin' stone
   But that's not how it used to be
   When the jester sang for the king and queen
   In a coat he borrowed from James Dean
   And a voice that came from you and me
   Oh and while the king was looking down,
   The jester stole his thorny crown
   The courtroom was adjourned,
   No verdict was returned
   And while Lenin read a book on Marx
   The quartet practiced in the park
   And we sang dirges in the dark
   The day the music died
   We were singin'...bye-bye... etc.

3. Helter-skelter in the summer swelter
   The birds flew off with a fallout shelter
   Eight miles high and fallin' fast,
   It landed foul on the grass
   The players tried for a forward pass,
   With the jester on the sidelines in a cast
   Now the half-time air was sweet perfume
   While the sergeants played a marching tune
   We all got up to dance
   But we never got the chance
   'Cause the players tried to take the field,
   The marching band refused to yield
   Do you recall what was revealed
   The day the music died
   We started singin'... bye-bye...etc.

4. And there we were all in one place,
   A generation lost in space
   With no time left to start again
   So come on, Jack be nimble, Jack be quick,
   Jack Flash sat on a candlestick
   'Cause fire is the devil's only friend
   And as I watched him on the stage
   My hands were clenched in fits of rage
   No angel born in hell
   Could break that Satan's spell
   And as the flames climbed high into the night
   To light the sacrificial rite
   I saw Satan laughing with delight
   The day the music died
   He was singin'...bye-bye...etc.

AND I LOVE HER

Words and Music by JOHN LENNON
and PAUL McCARTNEY

ANNIE'S SONG

Words and Music by
JOHN DENVER

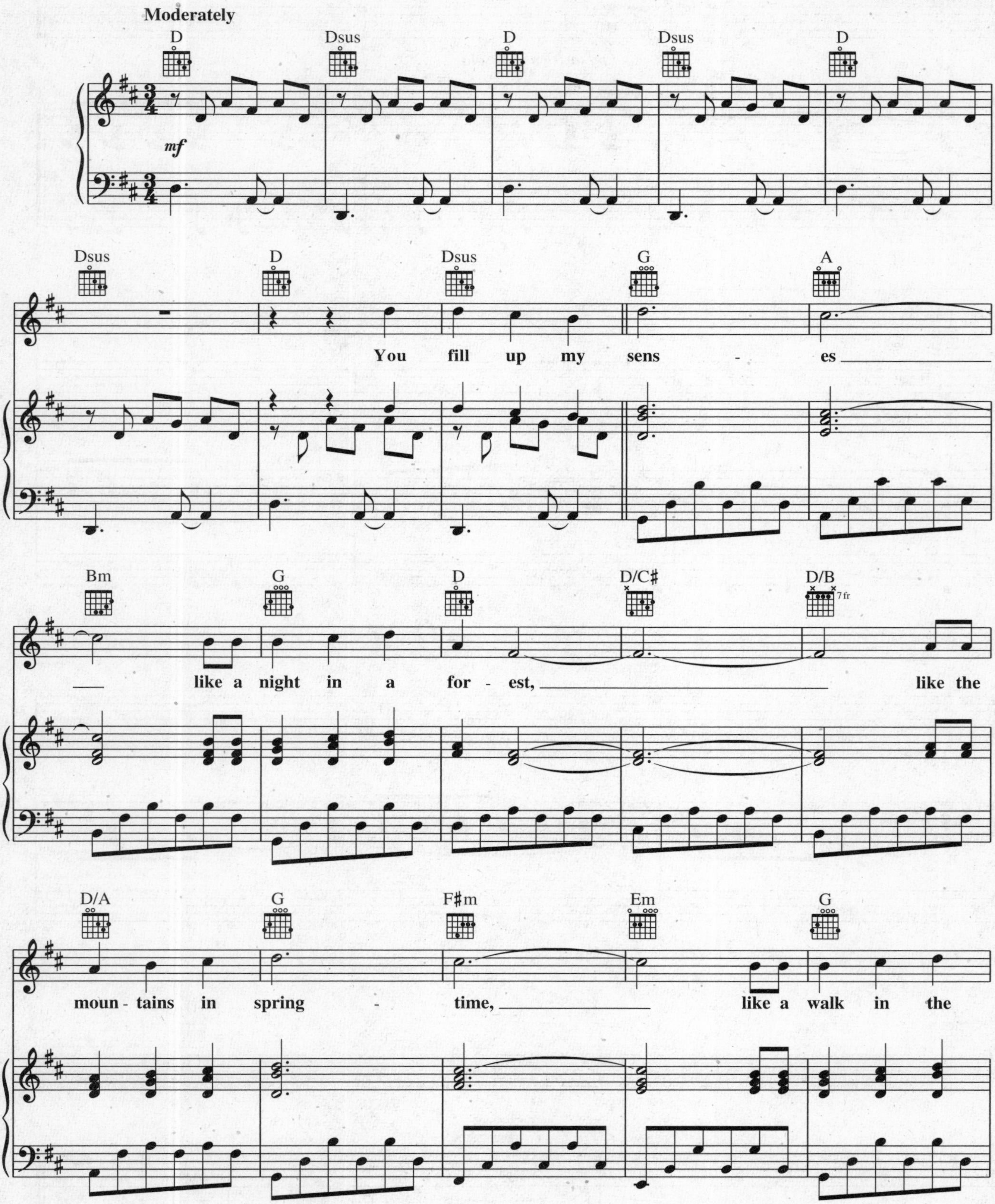

Moderately
D
Dsus
D
Dsus
D
mf
Dsus
D
Dsus
G
A
You fill up my sens - es
Bm
G
D
D/C#
D/B
7fr
like a night in a for - est,
like the
D/A
G
F#m
Em
G
moun - tains in spring - time,
like a walk in the

BARELY BREATHING

Words and Music by
DUNCAN SHEIK

BEST OF MY LOVE

Words and Music by JOHN DAVID SOUTHER,
DON HENLEY and GLENN FREY

Ev - 'ry night ___ I'm ly - in' in bed, ___ hold - in' you close ___ in my
Beau - ti - ful fac - es and loud emp - ty plac - es, look at the way that we

dreams; ___ think - in' a - bout ___ all the things that we ___ said ___ and
live; ___ wast - in' our time ___ on cheap talk and wine

BLAZE OF GLORY
featured in the film YOUNG GUNS II

Words and Music by
JON BON JOVI

wake up in the morn - ing and I raise my wea - ry head, ____ I've got an

night I go to bed, I pray the Lord my soul to keep. _ No, I ain't

BLACKBIRD

Words and Music by JOHN LENNON
and PAUL McCARTNEY

BLOWIN' IN THE WIND

Words and Music by
BOB DYLAN

Yes, and

Slower

rit.

BUS STOP

Words and Music by
GRAHAM GOULDMAN

CAN'T BUY ME LOVE

Words and Music by JOHN LENNON
and PAUL McCARTNEY

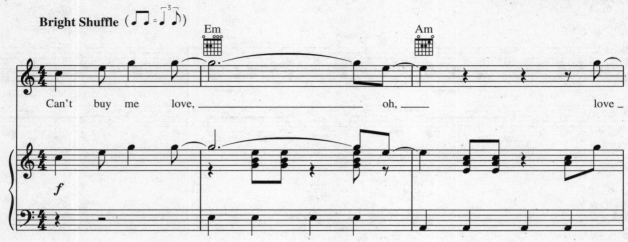

CHANGE THE WORLD

Words and Music by WAYNE KIRKPATRICK,
GORDON KENNEDY and TOMMY SIMS

If I can reach the __ stars, __
If I could be __ king, __

pull __ one down for you, __
e - ven for a day, __

COME MONDAY

Words and Music by
JIMMY BUFFETT

CRAZY ON YOU

Words and Music by ANN WILSON,
NANCY WILSON and ROGER FISHER

bod - y's in - sane? So a - fraid of one who's so a - fraid____ of you. What-cha

gon - na do?____

Ah...____

Ooh____ cra -

DEAR PRUDENCE

Words and Music by JOHN LENNON
and PAUL McCARTNEY

Dear _____ Pru - dence, _____
_____ Pru - dence, _____
_____ Pru - dence, _____

won't you come out to play? _____
o - pen up _____ your eyes. _____
let me see _____ you smile. _____

beau - ti - ful ___ and so are you. ___ Dear ___ Pru - dence, ___
you are part ___ of ev - 'ry - thing. ___ Dear ___ Pru - dence, ___
let me see ___ you smile a - gain. ___ Dear ___ Pru - dence, ___

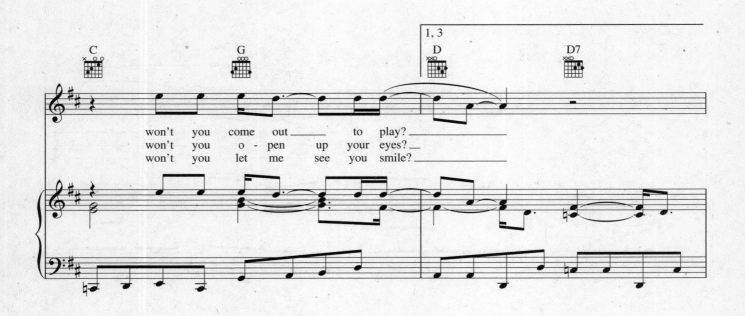

won't you come out ___ to play? _____
won't you o - pen up your eyes? _____
won't you let me see you smile? _____

Dear ___ ___

Look a-

FREE BIRD

Words and Music by ALLEN COLLINS
and RONNIE VAN ZANT

GIRL

Words and Music by JOHN LENNON
and PAUL McCARTNEY

HAVE YOU EVER
REALLY LOVED A WOMAN?

from the Motion Picture DON JUAN DeMARCO

Words and Music by BRYAN ADAMS,
MICHAEL KAMEN and ROBERT JOHN LANGE

1. To real-ly love a wom-an, _____ to un-der-
2., 3. *(See additional lyrics)*

stand her, _____ you got-ta know her deep in-side; _____ hear ev-e-ry

thought, _____ see ev-e-ry dream, _____ n' give her wings when she wants to

Additional Lyrics

2. To really love a woman, let her hold you
   Till ya know how she needs to be touched.
   You've gotta breathe her, really taste her.
   Till you can feel her in your blood.
   N' when you can see your unborn children in her eyes.
   Ya know ya really love a woman.

   When you love a woman
   You tell her that she's really wanted.
   When you love a woman
   You tell her that she's the one.
   Cuz she needs somebody to tell her
   That you'll always be together
   So tell me have you ever really,
   Really really ever loved a woman?

3. *Instrumental*

   Then when you find yourself
   Lyin' helpless in her arms.
   You know you really love a woman.

   When you love a woman *etc.*

HELPLESSLY HOPING

Words and Music by
STEPHEN STILLS

HER TOWN TOO

Words and Music by JOHN DAVID SOUTHER,
JAMES TAYLOR and ROBERT WACHTEL

HERE COMES THE SUN

Words and Music by
GEORGE HARRISON

Here comes the sun, here comes the sun, and I say, "It's all right."

To Coda

Sun,   sun,   sun,   here   it

comes.

D.S. al Coda

HOMEWARD BOUND

Words and Music by
PAUL SIMON

1. I'm sit-tin' in the rail-way sta-tion, got a tick-et for my
2. Ev-'ry day's an end-less stream_ of cig-a-rettes and
(3. To -) night I'll sing my songs a-gain,_ I'll play the game

dest-in-a-tion._____ Mm_____
mag-a-zines._____ Mm_____
and pre-tend._____ Mm_____

I WILL

Words and Music by JOHN LENNON
and PAUL McCARTNEY

I'LL HAVE TO SAY I LOVE YOU IN A SONG

Words and Music by
JIM CROCE

I'M LOOKING THROUGH YOU

Words and Music by JOHN LENNON
and PAUL McCARTNEY

Why, tell me why ___ did you ___ not treat me right? ___

Love has a nas - ty hab - it of

dis - ap - pear - ing o - ver - night. ___

You're think - ing
I'm look - ing through ___

IF YOU LEAVE ME NOW

Words and Music by
PETER CETERA

- row comes, ___ then we'll both ___ re - gret ___ the things we said ___ to - day. ___

To Coda ⊕

I'VE JUST SEEN A FACE

Words and Music by JOHN LENNON
and PAUL McCARTNEY

I've just seen a face, I can't for-get the time ___ or

JULIA

Words and Music by JOHN LENNON
and PAUL McCARTNEY

JUST A SONG BEFORE I GO

Words and Music by
GRAHAM NASH

LEAVING ON A JET PLANE

Words and Music by
JOHN DENVER

LONG LONG TIME

Words and Music by
GARY B. WHITE

LOST IN LOVE

Words and Music by
GRAHAM RUSSELL

re - al - ize__ the best__ part of love__ is the thin - nest slice__ and it don't__
(2-3) Lost in love__ and I don't__ know much.__ Was I think - ing a - loud__ and fell__

LOVELY RITA

Words and Music by JOHN LENNON
and PAUL McCARTNEY

me - ter   maid. __

NIGHT MOVES

Words and Music by
BOB SEGER

180

Strange how the night moves, __ with au-tumn clos-ing in. __

Tempo I

Night moves.
Lead vocal ad lib.

1-7

Night moves.

8

Vocal ad lib. continues

MAGGIE MAY

Words and Music by ROD STEWART
and MARTIN QUITTENTON

Moderately bright

ME AND BOBBY McGEE

Words and Music by KRIS KRISTOFFERSON
and FRED FOSTER

* *Vocal written one octave higher than sung.*

Lord.

MICHELLE

Words and Music by JOHN LENNON
and PAUL McCARTNEY

MORE THAN WORDS

Words and Music by NUNO BETTENCOURT
and GARY CHERONE

* Recorded a half step lower.

MY SWEET LORD

Words and Music by
GEORGE HARRISON

NORWEGIAN WOOD
(This Bird Has Flown)

Words and Music by JOHN LENNON
and PAUL McCARTNEY

NOWHERE MAN

Words and Music by JOHN LENNON
and PAUL McCARTNEY

Moderately

He's a real no - where man, sit - ting in his

no - where land, mak - ing all his no - where plans for

no - bod - y.

Does - n't have a
He's as blind as

world ___ is at your com - mand.
some - bod - y else lends you a hand.
world ___ is at your com - mand.

Instrumental
Does - n't have ___ a point of view, ___ knows not where he's
He's a real ___ no - where man, ___ sit - ting in his

(Instrumental)
go - ing to, ___ is - n't he ___ a bit ___ like you ___ and
no - where land, ___

OUR HOUSE

Words and Music by
GRAHAM NASH

PINK HOUSES

Words and Music by
JOHN MELLENCAMP

in - ter - state ___ run - nin' through ___ his front yard. ___ You know, he
greas - y hair ___ and a greas - y smile ___ that says, "Lord,
Go to work ___ in some high - rise and va - ca - tion down at

F   C   G

thinks he's got it so good. ___
this must be my des - ti - na - tion." ___
the Gulf of Mex - i - co. ___

And there's a
'Cause they
And there's

wom - an in the kitch - en clean - in' up the eve - nin' slop. ___
told me when I was young - er, "Boy, you gon - na be Pres - i -
win - ners and there's los - ers, but they ain't no big deal. ___

POETRY MAN

Words and Music by
PHOEBE SNOW

ROCKY MOUNTAIN HIGH

Words and Music by JOHN DENVER
and MIKE TAYLOR

He was born in the sum - mer of his
Ca - the - dral Moun - tains, he saw

twen - ty - sev - enth year, com - in' home to a
sil - ver clouds be - low, he saw ev - 'ry - thing as

place he'd nev - er been be - fore. He left
far as you can see. And they

POOR LITTLE FOOL

Words and Music by
SHARON SHEELEY

ROCKY RACCOON

Words and Music by JOHN LENNON
and PAUL McCARTNEY

help with good Rock - y's re - vi - val. _____

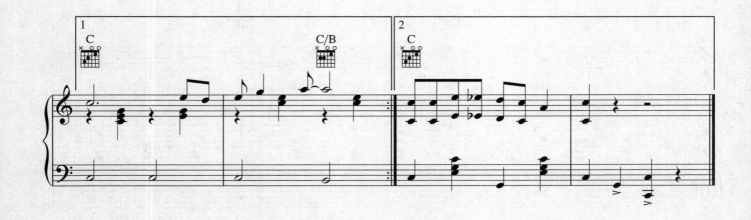

SHOW ME THE WAY

Words and Music by
PETER FRAMPTON

Moderately

I won - der how __ you're feel - ing. __ There's
I can see __ no rea - son. __ You're

RUNNING ON FAITH

Words and Music by
JERRY WILLIAMS

Slow Rock

Late-ly I been run-nin' on _____ faith. _____
Late-ly I been talk-in' in _____ my sleep.
Instrumental solo

(Sittin' On)
THE DOCK OF THE BAY

Words and Music by STEVE CROPPER
and OTIS REDDING

Moderate beat

Sit - tin' in the morn - ing sun,
left my ___ home ___ in Geor - gia
Sit - tin' here ___ rest - in' my bones, ___

I'll be
and this

sit - tin' when the eve - nin' ___ come. ___
head - ed for the Fris - co ___ bay. ___
lone - li - ness won't leave my a - lone.

Watch - in' the ships roll in, ___
I have ___ noth - in' to live ___ for,
Two thou - sand miles I roam ___

then I
look like
just to

SMALL TOWN

Words and Music by
JOHN MELLENCAMP

Well, I was born in a small ___ town,
Ed - u - cat - ed in ___ a small ___ town,

and I live in a small ___ town; prob -'ly die in a small ___
taught the fear of Je - sus in a small town; used to day dream in that

SOUTHERN CROSS

Words and Music by STEPHEN STILLS,
RICHARD CURTIS and MICHAEL CURTIS

STAY THE NIGHT

Words and Music by PETER CETERA
and DAVID FOSTER

one thing I can tell you, and per-fect-ly clear, we're gon-na have a ver-y good time.

Guitar solo-ad lib.

Solo ends

SUMMER BREEZE

Words and Music by JAMES SEALS
and DASH CROFTS

See the cur-tains hang-in' in the win-dow ___ in the eve-ning on a Fri-day night. ___
See the pa-per lay-in' on the side-walk, ___ a lit-tle mu-sic from the house next door. ___

___
___

A lit-tle light a shin-in' through the win-dow ___
So I walk on up to the door-step,

Repeat and Fade

SWEET TALKIN' WOMAN

Words and Music by
JEFF LYNNE

TAKE ME HOME, COUNTRY ROADS

Words and Music by JOHN DENVER,
BILL DANOFF and TAFFY NIVERT

TEARS IN HEAVEN

Words and Music by ERIC CLAPTON
and WILL JENNINGS

309

Be-yond the door ___ there's peace, I'm sure, _

THING CALLED LOVE
(Are You Ready For This Thing Called Love)

Words and Music by
JOHN HIATT

Don't have to hum-ble your-self __ to me; __
You ain't no i-con __ carved_ out-a soap

I ain't your judge or your king. __ And ba — by!
sent down here to clean up my rep-u-ta-tion. And ba — by!

You know you ain't no Queen of She - ba.
I ain't_ your_ Prince_ Charm-ing.

Ab
4fr
Bb7
Eb
3fr
comes from up a - bove.
I ain't no por - cu - pine,
Ab
4fr
Bb7
Eb
3fr
take off your kid gloves.
Are you read - y for a big
C7
G7
G5
3fr
Bb5
C5
3fr
F5
Play 4 times
thing called love?
G5
3fr
Bb5
C5
3fr
F5
G5
3fr
Bb5
Repeat and Fade
Just a cra - zy lit - tle thing called love.
Just a cra -

THIS LAND IS YOUR LAND

Words and Music by
WOODY GUTHRIE

TIME IN A BOTTLE

Words and Music by
JIM CROCE

TRAVELIN' MAN

Words and Music by
JERRY FULLER

VINCENT
(Starry Starry Night)

Words and Music by
DON McLEAN

Starry, starry night,
night,
night,

paint your pal - ette blue and grey.
flam - ing flow'rs that bright - ly blaze.
por - traits hung in emp - ty halls.

Look out on a sum - mer's day, with
Swirl - ing clouds in vio - let haze re -
Frame - less heads on name - less walls, with

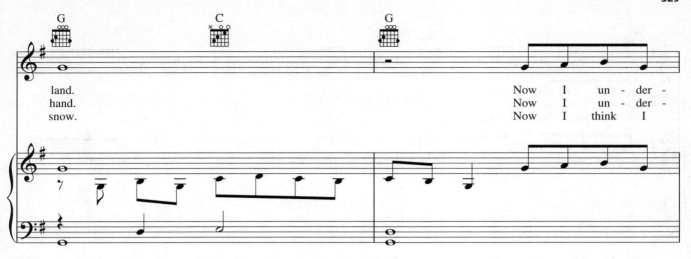

land.   Now I un-der-
hand.   Now I un-der-
snow.   Now I think I

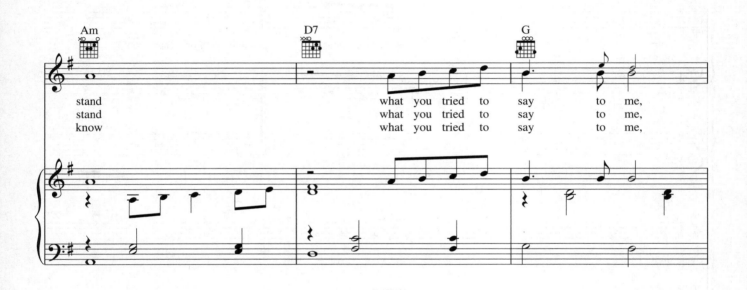

stand   what you tried to say   to me,
stand   what you tried to say   to me,
know   what you tried to say   to me,

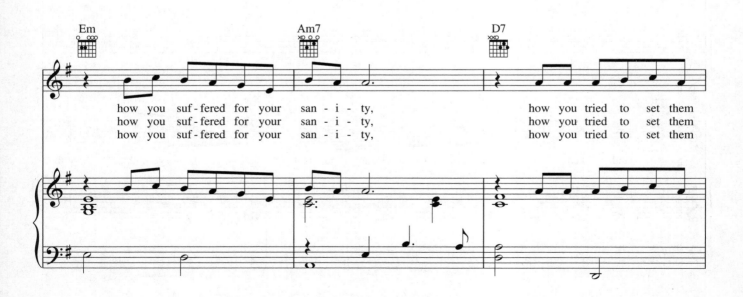

how you suf-fered for your san - i - ty,   how you tried to set them
how you suf-fered for your san - i - ty,   how you tried to set them
how you suf-fered for your san - i - ty,   how you tried to set them

UNTIL IT'S TIME FOR YOU TO GO

from ELVIS ON TOUR

Words and Music by
BUFFY SAINTE-MARIE

Moderately fast

You're not a dream, you're not an an-gel, you're a man.
dif-f'rent, worlds a - part, we're not the same,

I'm not a queen, I'm a wom-an, take my hand.
we laughed and played at the start like in a game.

We'll make a space in the lives that we'd planned,
You could have stayed out-side my heart but in you came,

WAKE UP LITTLE SUSIE

Words and Music by BOUDLEAUX BRYANT
and FELICE BRYANT

Rock Tempo

Wake up, Lit-tle Su - sie, ___ wake up.

We've both been sound a - sleep, ___ wake up ___
The mov-ie was-n't so hot, ___ it did-

WHERE HAVE ALL THE FLOWERS GONE?

Words and Music by
PETE SEEGER

tak - en hus - bands ev - 'ry one.   Oh, when   will they   ev - er

learn?   Oh,   when   will they ev - er   learn?

rit.   *p*

3. Where have all the young men gone? Long time passing.
   Where have all the young men gone? Long time ago.
   Where have all the young men gone?
   They're all in uniform.
   Oh, when will they ever learn?
   Oh, when will they ever learn?

4. Where have all the soldiers gone? Long time passing.
   Where have all the soldiers gone? Long time ago.
   Where have all the soldiers gone?
   They've gone to graveyards, every one.
   Oh, when will they ever learn?
   Oh, when will they ever learn?

5. Where have all the graveyards gone? Long time passing.
   Where have all the graveyards gone? Long time ago.
   Where have all the graveyards gone?
   They're covered with flowers, every one.
   Oh, when will they ever learn?
   Oh, when will they ever learn?

6. Where Have All The Flowers Gone? Long time passing.
   Where Have All The Flowers Gone? Long time ago.
   Where Have All The Flowers Gone?
   Young girls picked them, every one.
   Oh, when will they ever learn?
   Oh, when will they ever learn?

WONDERWALL

Words and Music by
NOEL GALLAGHER

YESTERDAY

Words and Music by JOHN LENNON
and PAUL McCARTNEY

Moderately, with expression

Yes-ter-day, ____
Sud-den-ly, ____

all my trou-bles seemed so
I'm not half the man I

far a-way, ____
used to be, ____

now it looks as though ___ they're
there's a shad-ow hang-ing